Red

the art of Chris

by Fr Bernard D. Green S.D.S.

All booklets are published thanks to the generous support of the members of the Catholic Truth Society

CATHOLIC TRUTH SOCIETY
PUBLISHERS TO THE HOLY SEE

Contents

The Situation

Complaints today about the moral chaos of our times are commonplace. “When I was young we never had to lock our doors. Neighbours looked out for each other”, “You can’t trust anyone anymore”. “Its come to something when you have to send your child to school in a bulletproof vest!”; “What ever happened to fidelity?” “Politicians are just a bunch of liars” And so the complaints go on.

A crucial dimension of this moral breakdown is the loss of shared moral standards. We have so emphasized the freedom of the individual to live as they want that we seem to have lost sight of the fact that to live together we also need a shared vision and values. No society can stand without a shared understanding of what is moral and what is not. At some level we have to share a common agreement as to what is good and bad. Without a common understanding of the nature and purpose of human life and what is good to pursue, we do not know what we can expect of one another and with that trust dies, wariness and fear increase, as does our inability to cooperate together.

This loss of common standards and the development of confused and contradictory moral attitudes and positions that characterizes our modern Western culture, is not just a result of circumstances. It is closely related to the cultural and philosophical assumption that there are no objective moral standards. Morality is seen as a matter of individual preference. Moral positions reflect the emotional desires of individual, not objective truth.

This relativism is related to our concept of freedom. It is part of our definition of freedom that each individual has the right to develop their own "lifestyle" and have this protected from encroachment from others. We deplore people "imposing" their moral standards upon us and try to prevent such people from gaining political power. Our moral focus is on safeguarding the freedom of the individual to live their own self-chosen values without let or hindrance from others.

It is on that basis that Hotel chains can make pornography available for their viewers and their guests. They are simply supplying a demand. They pass no moral judgment on what they show or on those who want to see them. The demand is there and so as good hoteliers, they feel bound to make it available. There is no moral judgment made here as to whether pornography is good or not. The practice is based solely on profit, and profit is morally neutral.

Moral Character and Law

The result of this loss of common ideas as to what is good and what is not is a chronic deterioration of informal social controls. A shared culture of moral values and disciplines in the past helped people to achieve self-discipline. Especially in moments of passion or temptation, they reinforced a person's ability to resist acting out his or her desires. Because something was generally disapproved of by the community, people thought twice about doing it. This is unfortunately no longer the case and the social motivation to impulse control has evaporated. People more and more act on impulse, satisfying their immediate whims and wishes. They become more and more unpredictable. Our social lives correspondingly become more chaotic and frightening.

Increasingly, the only source of impulse control that people have today is the fear of the law. It is the only framework of judgment by which they evaluate their behavior. They do not view their behavior in terms of morality but at best in terms of legality. For a good many people, wrong is simply the breaking of the civil or criminal code of law. When a politician or a businessman says: "I have done nothing wrong", he or she means that they have not broken the law. This, it seems, is all we have left. If we have any common standards, they come, not from a shared vision and set of values, but from that which is enshrined in law.

Is this bad? Does the law have any place in creating a better world? Clearly, yes. Good laws are essential to a good society and they have an important educative value. But, that value is limited. No matter how good laws may be, the fact is that we cannot create a world of joy and fullfilment based on 'not breaking a law.' Laws and their enforcement are necessary but they are not a cure for our moral sickness. Something more is needed.

What we don't need is more law enforcement, stiffer sentences, more prisons, but more people of moral character. We need people who are capable of living on the basis of objectively valid moral principles. We need people who are able to discriminate good ways of being human from bad. We need people who have a commitment to finding and living by principles that are deemed essential to our communal life. We need people who clearly understand that there is a difference between right and wrong and who try to find it. We need a social environment that motivates us to seek what is objectively right and wrong, that encourages us to delineate what is good for us all and what is bad for all.

What we need, then, is to create communities in which people can develop morally, growing up knowing a set of common values and standards, guided by living examples and disciplined by social expectations into living by them. In short, we have to create an environment that encourages the development of moral sensitivity and supports the discipline and sacrifice which being moral demands. Without this, the moral confusion will continue, and with it the sense of lostness that so afflicts people today.

And such is our society at the moment. We live in a culture that is morally adrift. We are no longer bound by a general sense as to the meaning and significance of human existence. The freedom that has been granted us by the loss of common standards is not leading to greater moral sensitivity but rather to its opposite. People are no longer thinking in objective moral terms but only in terms of what they personally and individually can get and get now. Moral sensitivity is dying among us and we risk raising a generation of moral illiterates.

Moral Character and Catholic Life

In this situation, Catholics, have an indispensable role to play. Above all other institutions of the Western world, the Catholic Church alone has the ability and resources to make a real difference in the moral climate of our time, and it is our mission to do so. In the Vatican II document, *Gaudium et Spes*, we are told that:

> The Christian who neglects his temporal duties neglects his duties towards his neighbour and even God, and jeopardizes his eternal salvation. (16)

Today, one of our most pressing of our temporal duties is to create a social environment in which all can live in peace and so flourish simply as human beings. Pope John Paul II challenged us to create a culture of life. A culture of life is one that affirms the intrinsic value of the individual from the moment he or she is conceived to the moment he or she departs this life naturally. He distinguished that from a culture of death that he saw increasingly gaining a hold of Western society. A culture of death is one in which killing others is the way to create a better world, so it is working to extend abortion, euthanasia, and assisted suicide.

John Paul challenged the whole Church to work in the world to build up a culture in which the individual dignity and life is safeguarded from conception to grave. We need, therefore, to ask ourselves whether we are fulfilling that role. How are we responding to the challenge?

This challenge is especially powerful at this time when we are being rocked by reports of bishops, priests and religious sexually molesting children. It is a time when we must reflect profoundly on how we are living morally. We were called out of the world to be a light in the darkness, a city set upon a hill for all to see and glorify God, and in doing so to make the reign of God present in our world. This is our vocation. We have to become a counter society to that which dominates our social and political life.

But, to what extent, do we stand out from our society as a people with shared moral standards that truly bring peace and joy to the human heart? Today we cannot avoid asking ourselves this question. Pope John Paul, in his travels around the world, consistently called us to do this. The *Catechism of the Catholic Church* has outlined our common faith and its moral requirements. It has made it clear what we stand for. We cannot say that we do not know. The *World Youth Days* around the world are continually demanding that we rise to the challenge of becoming what we are called to be. Our youth are demanding it. Now Pope Benedict has repeated the challenge, and he has addressed it to the whole world and the world is beginning to take notice. People are tired of living in a moral vacuum. It creates fear for the future. It betokens a fragmented, confused and incoherent life, and people do not want that. People generally are challenging us to understand our vision better and develop a way of life which flows coherently from it. They are thirsting for guidance in how to live well. They are looking for an example of a way of life that results in peace and joy. And the challenge is to us since we claim to be such a community.

The Virtue Tradition

Many theologians today believe that this can be found by a return to the past traditions. This is not simply nostalgia for some mythical perfect age gone by. Such has never existed. Rather, it is a desire to recapture a tradition which has been lost. This tradition combined a clear framework within which to think about moral behavior with the freedom to make those necessarily unique decisions that personal life demands. It looks to both objective guidelines for action and the subjective development of moral sensitivity.

The tradition is that of the virtues - the development of the theological virtues of faith, hope and love and the cardinal virtues of justice, courage, temperance and prudence.

The *Catechism of the Catholic Church* has placed these virtues at the core of the moral life (Pt 3. Art. 7). It tells us that the goal of the virtuous life is to become like God (Par 1803). God is the source of all life. God sustains life and promises us its total fulfillment. In the resurrection of Jesus from the dead, God has affirmed that life is victorious over death, that love seeks to give life. We are to be people who give, sustain and develop life. We are called to be a people whose own lives are in harmony with the purposes of God. We are to be a people who show forth the inner nature of God as the fullness of love and life.

This is the goal of the Catholic way of life: we are to witness as a community to the inner life of God Himself and we are to do so through living a life of virtue. Through the life of virtue we are to show the world what it means to be human. We are to make 'real' what it means to live and act like God in our world, and this we do by living the virtuous life.

The virtuous life was the basis of Catholic thinking about the moral life up until the late Middle Ages. It was then supplanted by an emphasis on simply being obedient to an external moral code, presented to us by authority. Being virtuous, then, meant living by the moral laws that had been laid down for us by those in authority. This is now recognized as being inadequate. Such obedience to moral norms does not of itself develop people of moral sensitivity. So the Church is now reaching back beyond this to the development of people who know what is right and wrong and who, by the grace of God are empowered to give themselves to realizing it.

The important phrase here is 'by the grace of God'. We need to recapture what that means if we are to realize our true vocation in the world: we are called to be a people who, through the grace of God, are able to become like God through living a virtuous life. We are called to witness to the world as to the power of God to bring our humanity to its fulfillment. This is something that has been re-emphasized in the *Catechism of the Catholic Church* by the very way in which it has organized its teaching on our way of life.

This modern statement of our faith and life sets the virtues in the context of the whole view of life provided by our faith. The section on Christian life is placed immediately after the section on the sacraments. The very arrangement tells us that our Christian life is not a matter of trying to be moral with the sacraments there to help. It is a matter of living from within a context of grace, with moral living flowing from that. It is our response of gratitude to God for first creating us and then redeeming us in Christ.

This location of the virtues in the context of grace makes the moral life of virtue something different from the way it was seen in the past. Virtue has in the past been given a rather bad name. It has almost been equated with self-righteousness. It was seen as the way in which, by our own efforts, we earn the approval of God and others and be rewarded in one way or another. The general impression we get of virtuous people is that they think of themselves as being morally superior to others. They are 'goodie-goodies' who are able to look down on others less good than themselves.

And there is always this danger with virtuous people unless they see themselves and their lives wholly within the context of grace. The context of grace tells us that, first of all, we are all sinners and that our salvation is the result of the gracious forgiveness of God for our moral failures both as a race and as individuals. Who is it that God approves of? It is not the one who is able to point to his or her good deeds but the one who above all else seeks the mercy of God for their sinfulness. Was this not the teaching of Jesus in the parable of the Pharisee and the Publican (*Lk* 18:9-18)?

Simply as human beings we all live within the ambit of God's merciful and compassionate love revealed to us in the life, death and resurrection of Christ. We are all sinners in need of redemption. That redemption was won for us by another. It is offered to us as a gift. It is this context of grace which guides and makes possible the life of virtue. We are virtuous because we wish to love as we have been loved. We wish to love as that love has been revealed to us in Christ. The writer of the First letter of John knew this, so he could write:

> We have come to know and to believe in the love God has for us. God is love, and whoever remains in love remains in God and God in him. In this is love brought to perfection among us, that we have confidence on the day of judgment because as he is, so are we in this world. There is no fear in love, but perfect

> love drives out fear because fear has to do with punishment, and so one who fears is not yet perfect in love.
>
> We love because he first loved us. If anyone says, "I love God," but hates his brother, he is a liar; for whoever does not love a brother whom he has seen cannot love God whom he has not seen. This is the commandment we have from him: whoever loves God must also love his brother. (*1 Jn* 4:16-21)

We love as we have been loved, and that love, the love that is divine, has been revealed to us through the death and resurrection of Jesus. It is a quality of love that is willing to give one's life away for one's enemies. There can be no higher ideal. It is an ideal imbued with the power of life itself. It is a love that acts to give life, to safeguard life, to make life for others possible.

In this context we can see the true meaning of virtue. The word itself comes from the Latin *vir-viris* which means man. *Virtus-utis* from that root means strength. A virtuous person is one who is strong in doing good. A virtuous person is like a great oak in the storm that stands strong and endures. A non-virtuous person is like a leaf in a breeze, blown this way and that. The strong and virtuous person is at peace within him or herself. Their desires are integrated around long-term goals. He or she has a sure aim in life and their lives make sense. The non-virtuous person, on the other hand, lives a chaotic and disturbed life, constantly pulled this way and that, confused and getting into trouble because their desires are contradictory.

And the foundation of a virtuous person's life is the bedrock of humility, which means an open-eyed acknowledgment and self-acceptance in both their good points and in their weaknesses and failures. They know their own need for divine assistance if they are to stay strong and live strong and coherent lives. They do not rest their ability to be virtuous on their own strength but on the strength of the Spirit that God has given them. They believe in and trust the power of God who created them and who redeemed them in Christ, to guide and uphold them in becoming truly who God wishes them to be.

The Theological virtues

Because of this basic context of grace, the foundations of the Christian life of virtue are the theological virtues: **faith, hope and charity**. These are primary. Without them we cannot be fulfilled as human beings.

Faith

Faith is the bedrock. Faith makes life and growth, change and development possible because it affirms that all of life is intelligible. Without this underlying understanding of life, human growth and development is impossible. All human beings affirm by their actions that life is meaningful and significant. It is something built into human nature. To live is worthwhile. It can bring satisfaction and fulfillment. Mankind of its very nature seeks that happiness and fulfillment. Even atheists affirm the intelligibility and significance of the human pursuit of happiness through living a moral life.

What Christianity adds to this natural pursuit is a profound justification for living it. As Christians we live in a world which makes sense because it comes to us from a loving and merciful God who is present with us in all our struggles. God became human and "dwelt amongst us". He dwelt among us and raised our humanity up to a totally new level of fulfillment. He revealed to us what it means to be fully human. In Christ he revealed to us our own divine possibilities. He revealed Himself to us in his holiness. He revealed that holiness is a matter of being willing to sacrifice oneself for the good of our enemies. In Christ on the cross we see love revealed. In Christ resurrected we see what love can accomplish: our destiny is revealed. This is the content of our **faith**. It flows out of a profound belief in God as love.

Out of this faith, prayer emerges naturally. In prayer we relate ourselves personally to the One who gave us life, sustains it in existence and has acted to redeem it from sin. The central basis of prayer is pure adoration. In adoration we acknowledge God as the center of all existence. We 'hallow' his name. We affirm our own creaturehood.

We acknowledge that we ourselves are not the center of reality. We acknowledge that there is a purpose to this world and to natural life that transcends us. We seek to harmonize ourselves with that purpose. It grounds, then, the bedrock virtue of humility. In faith we affirm both that we are limited in our capacities, yet that we have capacities given us that can be at the service of life. We acknowledge both our limitations and our potential as life-givers.

Hope

Because of our faith, we are able to live, therefore, in a profound **hope** that, despite the negative and limiting conditions of this life, we will be able to share in that fulfillment through our faithful relationship with God. Such a hope is very difficult in a world without God. Natural life, life in the concrete so-to-speak, cannot justify such a hope. It is there, and people do live out of hope, but it is blind. If natural life would tell us anything it is that there is a tragic quality to human existence that we are of ourselves unable to overcome. Natural life is permeated with the desire for fulfillment but of itself cannot satisfy that desire.

We search for it through possessing things, having a variety of experiences, and undertaking satisfying work. But, not only do these not satisfy our longing for fulfilment but death brings them to an end. 'Natural' death truncates our desire for fulfilment, rendering it 'absurd'. Furthermore, human existence is now vulnerable to a particular form of 'unnatural' death: death through the deliberate will of another. This vulnerability, in Catholic thought is the consequence of an original 'sin'. This sin resulted in that peculiar form of death we call murder. It is portrayed in Genesis in the story of Cain and Abel as the first fruits of the original moral failure. If there is one dimension of human existence now that renders our search for fulfillment in this life 'absurd' it is our vulnerability, realized more and more every day in our present condition, of an unnatural death at the hands of others either through their callous indifference or deliberate malice. The terrorist is the symbol, though by no means the only expression of this tragic element of human existence.

Life in this world, natural life, now lies in the shadow of this tragic element. It forms the ever-present background to human striving. Today, our vulnerability to this has issued in a massive preoccupation with security. We live in a continual state of anxiety. It threatens and mocks all efforts to create a perfect world.

This tragic character of human existence weakens man's capacity to live in hope. It remains a blind affirmation in the face of the evidence. The Christian is rescued from this blind hope to one securely based in empirical reality: the defeat of sin and death in the crucifixion and resurrection of Jesus. Because in the resurrection, God is revealed as total faithfulness, our natural hope is surely grounded. Nothing can shake it, not even the worst of evils. All happens within the ambit of divine purpose. Relying not on their own strength and competence but on the Spirit of God within them, Christians are able to give themselves over to the demands of their lives and the challenges it brings in confidence of success. It makes growth and development as a human being possible.

Love

It is this hope which empowers us to reach out to the world and others with the deepest possible

love, affirming the eternal significance of every individual and able to work sacrificially for their fulfillment in imitation of Jesus the Christ.

By 'sacrificially', it is meant that we are able to give up opportunities for personal satisfactions now in order to realize good for others. This is what Jesus did throughout his life and especially on the cross. As with him so with the follower of Jesus, the good of others dominates their motivations and projects. It's most profound expression and its paradigm is love for our enemies and the capacity to do good to those who hate us. Jesus, himself, summed it up in the admonition: Love the Lord your God with your whole mind and heart and your neighbour as yourself (*Lk* 10:27)

Through such a love, which reaches the humanity of others in all its sinfulness, we grow in our recognition of others as individuals and as members of the community. Through this love as Christians we are able to seek ever-deeper union with the other simply as human. We go beyond loving those bound by relationships of blood, culture, race and status simply to the human.

This love is concretized in love for the poor, who can give us nothing in return, and love of one's enemies, who will not give us love, or even thanks, in return. The only criterion by which we determine how to relate to others is simply human need. We seek their good and hold ourselves to what is good for them in the face of rejection.

But, in this notion of love, is the most profound understanding of the nature of God: God as Trinitarian. It is the belief that God is a community of life. This belief in God as Trinitarian grounds the Catholic way of seeing human beings and justifies the basis of the Catholic way of life as one of learning how to love so that we might be able to enter into eternal life.

In this, Christian life flies in the face of the empirical. It affirms that love and life go together. There is nothing in natural life that could ground such a belief. The evidence tells us rather that loving others will not necessarily result in a better life, and Darwinism tells us that life goes together with domination and the survival of the strongest, yet revelation tells us that life comes through giving love rather than taking or receiving it.

Loving others does not always mean getting it right. We can love others and still do that which harms them.

Furthermore, we can love others and still evoke their hatred. Such is quite a common human experience. Yet we continue to affirm that love and life go together. The Beatles educated a whole generation to believe that "All you need is love". And they were right. But, they did not tell us what that love was and how it might give life. Christianity does. It reveals to us what real love is and that there is an ultimate link between them: Jesus loved in the most profoundly self-sacrificial way and it was because of this that he was raised from the dead. In Jesus, we see revealed that love and life do ultimately go together and knowing this, the Christian can love in the same way as Jesus did. Such loving is not irrational but makes sense ultimately. We now know the fundamental characteristic of love: its ability to sacrifice for the good of the other, even our enemy.

However, while the theological virtues are the way in which we bring ourselves into a direct relationship with the God who has revealed

Himself to us in Jesus Christ, and are made possible in us by His grace, they do not of themselves tell us how to live in this world or what to do.

Unfortunately, it is very easy to be committed to the notion of love, to be in love with love, so to speak, but, in fact, not act in a very positive way towards others. We can confuse intention with being. I may want to be good and have every intention of being good but in fact do and am evil. We will often be puzzled at ourselves and what we do. We are not bad people and we love others, so why did we do what we did! I do not know what came over me we might say. St. Paul captured this experience when he said:

> What I do, I do not understand. For I do not do what I want, but I do what I hate. (*Rm* 7:15)

What, he asked, could rescue him from that debilitating condition. The answer is the life of the cardinal virtues. It is these that move us from ideal to practice. It is the way in which we actually become real lovers, rather than people who simply love the ideal.

It is here, then, that the Cardinal virtues become important. They enable us to truly love and so become good. They move us from inner intention to external action. They form the inner person in such a way that their external behavior is good and good consistently, not just spasmodically as with most of us. Through virtuous actions we truly become good, we become "sensible" people, people who consistently act in a reasonable way. We become wise.

A "wise" person, and we all admire such, is a virtuous person. And it is to wisdom that our faith calls us. From the beginning the Christian emphasis has always been on character as being the primary constituent of the moral life rather than mere obedience to complex behavioral law. There are in fact relatively few direct behavioral prescriptions in the New Testament. The emphasis is on the quality of the inner life of the person. It was concerned with the condition of a person's heart. What were the basic attitudes and values which a person should espouse to live well? This was the primary concern and this is the primary thrust of the **Cardinal virtues**.

The Cardinal Virtues

These **Cardinal virtues** were developed first by Greek moralists. They looked at the sort of person who would truly achieve happiness because all the major demands of their being would be harmonized and disciplined. Living these virtues brings moral integrity into a person's life.

In the Greek framework, there are four basic habits of living needed to be cultivated if a person was to truly be happy and, if we reflect upon ourselves in the light of them, we will see how right they were. The Church adopted them precisely because they met the need for the development of a wise heart. It has revived them now precisely for the same reason. In the environment of moral confusion in our times, do we not yearn for people who are just and religious, temperate, courageous and prudent?

These are the qualities we associate with a loving character because they integrate five main dimensions of human being and becoming:

1. the need to integrate ourselves with the transcendent through prayer and worship (**religion**);
2. the need to integrate ourselves as individuals with the wider community (**justice**);
3. the need to hold ourselves to the difficult task of realizing what is good no matter what the risks involved (**courage**);
4. the need to integrate our various desires into a hierarchy of importance (**temperance**);
5. and the need to make personal decisions as to how to live out the requirements of the above goals within the specific and particular circumstances of our historical situation (**prudence**).

Justice

The first set of virtues concerns our relationships to others. Through **justice** we generate the principles of communal living, inhibiting the instinct to self-centeredness. Through thinking justly we generate those principles of communal living to which as individuals we must hold ourselves to no matter what our personal inclinations might be.

Our culture has seemingly reduced that law of justice down to one: everyone has the freedom to develop his or own moral code and all must be tolerant of the different life-styles that result. In this context tolerance is the primary virtue that needs to be lived if we are to flourish as human beings. With this emphasis on tolerance, a wedge has been formed between truth and freedom. Freedom is understood to be the ability to decide for oneself what is right and wrong. Freedom is no longer grounded on the ability to do what is right but rather on the ability to choose what one thinks is moral.

In the moral confusion of our times Catholic thought asserts, through the virtue of justice, that there are objective norms of right and wrong. Life is not simply a 'do as you please' affair. Morality is not simply an individual matter of preference but a matter of objective standards and values which we must all adhere to if we are to live together in peace and harmony. A just person searches these out and lives them. As he realizes the virtue of justice, so he grows in freedom: freedom and doing what is right are intrinsically dependent on each other.

Religion

Through the virtue of **religion**, considered by the ancients as a special form of justice, we acknowledge our essential creaturehood and dependence on God for salvation and so discipline the tendency to try to be God. This is so difficult for us today. We hate submission. We do not like to think that there is anything or any person higher than ourselves. We now possess god-like powers and we need to be willing to enter into our new status as God.

At worst then, we wish to be considered as God. That is right or wrong which I say is right or wrong. We are approaching the time when we can determine what sort of human beings we want to be. We will soon be able to design our own selves and our own children. We may even through the act of cloning store up for ourselves parts for transplant that enable us to escape natural death.

At best, we are prepared to see God as a partner in our self-determined projects. We invoke his allegiance to our projects. How many sportsmen do we hear say after a victory: "God was with me, tonight". There is an alliance forged between us and God which renders us equals.

Both these stances are bound up with the protection and affirmation of our ego. They affirm the ego as against God. It is an ego that our culture wishes to promote and cultivate. It aims at creating the autonomous man and that autonomous man is subject to no laws beyond the ones he seeks to impose on himself. What morality he wishes to live by is a morality that he or she develops.

Genuine religion, the Christian religion especially, through its various practices of worship, challenges us to recognize the essential transcendence of God to ourselves, our origins as lying in the will of God, and our destiny as subject to His grace. It calls us to see morality as having an objective character and as binding on all human being. This nature was given to us by God as our creator. We are ordered to obeying that morality and in doing so to worship God as other than ourselves.

This differentiation is very important to our growth and development as human beings. Only if we see God as transcendent to ourselves can we relate to the Divine as the source of existence and of its destiny and fulfillment. God thereby becomes the beacon of our becoming, enabling us to accept our essential ignorance of the mystery of life. He enables us also to be open to its unfolding reality, ever able to change and develop to something new under its impact. The acts of the virtue of religion are therefore essential to genuine human growth and happiness.

Temperance

This second set is concerned with our relationship to ourselves. Through **temperance**, we restrain our immediate wants to make possible a style of life capable of realizing our long-term needs. It enables us to integrate our manifold desires and bring order into the various pleasures of life by seeing to what extent they are capable of satisfying our desire for fulfillment. We are thereby able to avoid illusion about the varied pleasures of life and to expect of things and people more than they can give.

What temperance rescues us from is addiction. Addiction results when we seek our total fulfillment through some natural good. When we seek endless moments of the satisfaction from some natural good, then we are addicted, and we can be addicted to anything: drink, drugs, sex, money or political power. We can look for total satisfaction in any of these areas, and because they cannot deliver the sort of fulfillment we want of them, they have to be endlessly repeated. We become preoccupied with their satisfaction. We seek more and more of what cannot of its nature satisfy us. We are locked into a blind alley that is going nowhere.

Temperance is the virtue that enables us to order our pleasures and see them realistically. We are not blinded by our immediate desires and so diverted from that which will truly realize our fulfillment. We can look beyond the moment to our long-term good and live for that now. This virtue places us directly in opposition to our culture today which encourages and tries to make possible the quickest possible impulse satisfaction. You should be able to get what you desire right now, immediately, without delay. Why should we surprised if our children take the criminal way to quick and easy money, or take drugs as a way of achieving effortless pleasure and ecstasy?

Courage

Through **courage** one holds in check the fear of losing one's being in order to give oneself over to that which is noble and good in spite of the sacrifices it might demand. Courage, then, enables us to reach for that which is higher when the occasion for it emerges. It therefore enables us to sustain our long-term efforts to realize something of higher value in life. It sustains our ability to enter in the process of growth and development and overcome the fear of death that surrounds it. Our yearning for this shows itself constantly in the desire for heroes. Heroes put their lives on the line in a self-sacrificing way. They look to what is noble and hold themselves to it no matter what. That we admire.

But as a virtue courage is most applicable to the demands of everyday life. It is something each one of us are faced with as we make moral choices. To live by the principles of Catholic faith, today, is going to require ever stronger courage as secularism grows stronger around us.

Prudence

Finally, through **prudence** one is able to live out these various dimensions of human existence in a way that takes careful account of the possibilities open to us within the concrete circumstances of our lives. It enables us to examine ourselves as unique persons living within circumstances and situations that offer specific possibilities and exclude others. Being present to them, we alone can discern what precisely is possible for us in the here and now in the light of long-term goals. Prudence is the virtue that enables us to decide how to realize those goals and discover the resources necessary to act on our decisions.

This is contrary to a common understanding of prudence as the virtue of being cautious. Prudence is in fact the virtue of sensible risk-taking. It means being able to take personal responsibility for one's decisions and actions. In an age in which "nobody is to blame", when the common refrain is: "It was not my fault", this is the virtue of moral and psychological maturity. In being prudent all the other virtues are brought to concrete expression. No wonder in the Middle Ages when the life of virtue was more central to the Church's moral thinking that it was known as *"the"* virtue.

Conclusion

In this tradition of virtue, then, placed within the overall vision of Christian faith with its challenge to the highest quality of love for others realized only through grace, we have a powerful means to meet the moral confusion of our age. By recovering this tradition we should be able to develop people who are virtuosos in living and witnesses to the power of grace. They are, principled yet flexible, disciplined yet not rigid. They are people who can enjoy life and its pleasures yet are courageously able to sacrifice it for a higher value if so required.

More than ever today we need people who respect themselves and can give the same respect to others, people who in doing good for others find their own self-realization. It is for us to rediscover the environment of grace within which these virtues can be developed. Recovering virtue and virtuous living is central to our salvific mission to our world at this time.